Laying By

Laying By

poems

Vincent Wixon

FLOWSTONE PRESS
Illinois Valley, Oregon

FLOWSTONE PRESS

Laying By
Copyright © 2017 Vincent Wixon

Front cover image and interior images
by R. Eric Stone (rericstone.com)

Author photo by Pam Danielle (pamdaniellephotography.com)

First Flowstone Press Edition • October 2017
ISBN 978-1-945824-09-8

for Patty

and in memory of Peter Sears
(1937-2017)

and Ralph Salisbury
(1926-2017)

Table of Contents

I. Prairie State

Fall Plowing	5
At the Threshing Bee	6
Idle	7
Perspective	8
Bethel Cemetery	9
Scene in Black and Gray	10
Weight	11
Ground Blizzard on the Prairie	12
In the Hayloft	13
Fox Crossing	14
Drive-by	15
Driver's Ed	16
Fourth-hand	17
In the Classroom	18
Shore	19
Blue Moon	20
Pike	21

II. Pacific Slope

The Meadow	25
Keepsake	26
Pacific Coast	27
Primary Season	28
Church Street	29
Castoffs	30
Backyard	31
Mid-May	33
Air Conditioning	34
Autumnal	35
Apocalypse	36
Vision	37
Tracks	38
Deeper	39
The Routine at Stonesthrow Ranch	40
Open	41

III. Afield

Ancient Ones	45
What the Dead Miss	46
Goodbye to the Tears	47
Call	48
Legacy	49
Insomnia	50
Hostage	51
Redrock	52
Recent Reading	53
Silk	54
The Words	55
Portal	56
Outlet	57
Parallel	58
Stonework	59
Implications	60
Watcher	61
Lost	62

IV. Return

Return	67
Cold Spell	68
Ticking	69
Tinnitus	70
Calling	71
Rust	72
Work	73
Endings	74
Siblings in August	75
Decluttering	76
Element	78
Empathy	79
Encounter	80
Wings	81
Father and Son	83
Close	85
Thirst	86
Acreage	87

Laying By

a. *plowing between rows of a crop, such as corn or soybeans, to loosen soil and dig out weeds for the final time of the season*

b. *putting away for future use*

I.

Prairie State

Fall Plowing

Topsoil scours off the shares and glistening moldboards,
oily and black as cinders.

Oat stubble folds under,
clods tumble back into troughs the tilling leaves.

The governor kicks in.
The old Allis strains
to pull three bottoms.

Thirty years of that would make anyone deaf.

Fall is in the air, the sun angled and warm,
nights cool.

Behind the plow in the middle of the country,
ring-billed gulls amass on the black soil,
gorging on what's turned over.

At the Threshing Bee

At the threshing bee old farmers in bib overalls
grip three-tined pitchforks,
and, after a time, the rhythm comes back,
shoulders loosen,
hands blister where calluses once shone.

Pulled by a Farmall H coated with dust and chaff,
the wagon lurches across the field,
tires snapping the stubble.

The old men drift alongside,
tossing the bundles aboard in one tempered motion,
as though dancing with smooth, thin partners.

Idle

The seasonal flowers are lovely—
purple asters and fall crocuses,
but the rain makes it hard on farmers,
who'd have paid big money for it in August.
Midmorning they shake dice for coffee at the Red Rooster;
their enormous combines stand idle in the fields.

In the afternoon the farmers linger in open doors
of machine sheds, grease guns in hands,
looking west for signs of clearing. Rain
drips off the eaves, cutting little furrows.
The flowers are indistinct purple smudges
under the trees.

Perspective

           1.
The girl wearing a ribbon in her hair,
a cotton dress and galoshes
scowls into the camera.
She has her hands on the shoulders of her little sister
as if she would drive her into the ground
like a posthole digger.

That force has not yet registered on the sister's round face
surrounded by a halo of light hair, which my mother hated,
and when my aunt was a baby in the crib
stuffed a sock in her mouth
to shut her up.

           2.
Later, and until their deaths, they were inseparable,
though my aunt drank and smoked and had 7-Up and ice cream
and a television,
and stayed up late watching Jack Paar.
I could too when I slept over,
but I loved my mother
and sat beside her in the pew.

           3.
Around them the scrubby, muddy lawn
not yet restored to life,
and the hedge of spirea, beat up from breaking snow,
are staggering into spring.

In the distance those landmarks of the prairie—
grain elevator and water tower—
loom in perfect geometry.

Bethel Cemetery

I dreamed we escaped from our graves,
crawled under the fence, and tumbled down the ravine.
We looked at each other in our best suits and prettiest dresses,
happy we weren't wearing shoes,
delighted to unclasp our hands,
surprised to still be wearing glasses
and how clean they were.
Never when alive could we see so clearly.

After trudging the gravel roads
under a blazing sun and hazy blue sky,
past the emerald corn and soybean fields,
our feet began to blister, our clothes grew limp,
but the mosquitos left us alone.
We carried the little ones who began to fuss.

The farther we got from Bethel
the more we began to miss it—up there on the hill,
the cool breeze soughing across the grass and stones,
the call of familiar birds in the trees.
Even the startling rifle salutes on Memorial Days
had become familiar. We began to talk it over.
We knew where we were better off.

Scene in Black and Gray

Blackbirds become a swirling blanket
and descend to a giant cottonwood
in the grove of a ruined farm.

Planted a century ago,
the tree is splintered, nearly dead.
Bark in large sheets is piled
around the base.

The barns and sheds are the same gray
as the tree and the owl in the hayloft.
Nettles thread the frozen chains and gears
of the seeder, harrow, and plow.

The birds rest on a slight rise
among thousands of picked acres
scattered with bins and silos
fading into haze.

For a time the flock blackens the snags,
then lifts and flies off, pulsing
as one thing.

Weight

Show me a person who doesn't die
and I'll show you a ghost passing
through the walls of the house
to wander the farmyard.

He wants to hang around the family,
but no longer pulls his weight.
Some chores go untended. A younger brother
inherits feeding the chickens, collecting eggs.

He senses the ghost beside him in the coop,
his anguish, but soon has had enough.
"Go haunt Grace at the ironing board.
The hens won't lay with you around."

At mealtime the ghost lingers in the pantry,
hungry for his chair at the table. The family
keeps a steady chatter, passes plates,
and gnaws at what may have chanced
after the tractor turned over on him.

Finally, the youngest faces him.
"Ernest," she says, "you have to leave now.
You're no use to us." He nods his pale head
and glides off past the honey separator
and through the screen door.

What does the girl feel? She sighs, goes back
to the dining room, picks up a spoon,
and eats her pudding. The others stare
at their empty bowls. It tastes good to her.

Ground Blizzard on the Prairie

Snow fills the ditches
level with the roads,
and the ditches, fields, and roads
merge into one plane
in a land with few hills.

Only fence posts
mark the boundaries
where fields begin,
and shredded plastic bags
on the wires signal
where the wind blows,
and how hard,

along with horned larks
that rise in flocks from the roadside
and sail sideways
until their wings take hold
and they right themselves
and scatter east along with
everything else unanchored.

And the people,
those who have to be out—
faces layered against cutting ice—
bend into it,
grope across the crusted banks
to the barn and the animals
that depend on them.

In the Hayloft

I can hear the cows below stamp their feet
in their stalls, the clang of milk cans,
and the evening rosary from KMHL Radio—
Hail Mary, full of grace, the Lord is with thee.

The cows' devotion,
my father's attendance on them morning and night,
and the warmth of their bodies and breath
sift up through the shrunken boards of the hayloft
as I work on my shot in the dim light from a bulb in the rafters.

We all have our rituals.
Mine are ten set shots from the free throw line painted white,
ten jump shots from the angles, from the baselines—
hardly any room on the right before my back hits the wall.

Snow blows through the cracks
around the door shaped like a tongue.
Sparrows rustle on the metal rail running under the peak.
A litter of kittens is hidden away in the bales.
In a week or so they'll emerge mewing and blinking.

I shoot, lost in the rhythm of dribble, rise up,
cradle the ball on fingertips, hands above my head,
release with a flick of the wrist,
lick my fingers for the slick ball, and rise up again.

Later, I'll climb down from the loft
and make my way to the house. In the barnyard
snowflakes swirl, a constellation in the mercury light,
and the wind takes my breath away.

Fox Crossing

Just as my brother said,
late in the day a red fox
trotted along the edge of the lawn
near a twenty foot drop
to the shore of Lake Mendota.

It paused, right forepaw raised,
plumed tail horizontal, a counterweight.
and looked at me watching
through the long window
of the living room.

Then it lowered its paw
and trotted on at the same pace,
not hurried, but purposeful,
until it disappeared
behind a neighbor's shrub.

Beyond where the fox had been,
through alders, the lake
gathered the last of daylight.
A line of cormorants filed low
across the surface.

I wondered where the fox
was headed—from a den to hunt
or back empty-jawed.
How did it live so close to houses
and gardens and mowed lawns,

gracing us with its red, compact body,
sharp nose and ears and self-possession,
unafraid—a surprise, like its musky scent
lingering at the drop-off.

Drive-by

Beyond the wire fence a boy
holds a strap attached to a horse.

In white shirt and dark pants,
the boy stands nearly at attention.

The horse is chestnut
with white stockings and blaze.

They disappear as my car rounds
a curve through a gauntlet of cottonwoods.

Shade then sun then shade,
then a straightaway.

I believe the boy and the horse
have stood that way for a long time.

Between them the strap is slack.

Driver's Ed

When the pickup started to slide,
I didn't panic, but pumped the brakes,
as taught in Driver's Ed by Mr. Robbins,
who'd fought in Korea and paddled boys in study hall,
and, when I pulled out in front of a Fairlane,
stomped on the passenger-side brake of the '58 Chevy,
then called me a dumb cluck.

Mr. Robbins,
his waxy crew cut and red face,
the dark green hulking car . . .

My foot moved rhythmically.
The car continued to glide,
slewed 90 degrees, and nosed into an elm,
like a boat easing against a piling.

That should have been set to a waltz,
I thought, as I gazed at the bare patch
on the tree trunk and shifted into reverse.
The sandbags over the rear tires would help.
I needed purchase. Easing down the gas pedal,
I backed into the street.

Fourth-hand

A high school classmate
didn't recognize me without my baseball cap.
When I put it on the doubt left her eyes.
"You haven't changed a bit," she said.

She said she last saw me running down a fly ball
on senior skip day. I reached
across my body with my left hand, lunged,
and closed it like a book.

I could see her in her cheerleader outfit,
all those years ago,
pleated skirt the size of a face towel,
V-neck sweater with the block T
plastered across her chest,
sweat sheen on her forehead.

Her letter sweater smelled musty,
like mine, folded beside old trophies
on a shelf in an upstairs closet—
a hand-me-down from my brother,
who bought it from a teammate,
his name stitched inside.
Already a third-hand sweater
I passed on to my granddaughter.

She dragged it on, blonde hair and eager face
appearing through the hole. "Go Scrappers!"
she cried, legs apart, one hand on a hip,
the other thrust toward the ceiling.

In the Classroom

Brown and green tiles in the hall march into the classroom
and square the rows of desks, screwed to long boards to lock them down.
My crepe-soled shoes squeak toward mine, back with the others
at the alphabet's tail end. My shoes feel good, springy—
brown leather and laces Uncle Bill taught me to tie
with the bow straight across.

I push the desk lid up and down to hear the creak
and reveal my books, my pulp pad, and box of crayons.
Light coming through the ink hole makes a bright spot
on my reader. From up front beneath the flag
a sharp voice jars my reverie.

Lid in place and my elbows on its slanting brown top,
I play my index finger along the carved initials
of my predecessors, those allowed to carry jackknives
and spread compasses. There's a mysterious stain,
bat wings around the ink hole. It smells like chalk
and floor wax in here. Above the blackboard President Washington
inspects the second half of the alphabet written in Palmer hand.

I can read, and that's what I care about—books of boys
barely making the team then sinking the crucial shot,
cowboy stories, horse books though I've never ridden a horse,
tales of sled dogs in the far north and those who save lives
or get lost and find their way home. I do my school work
and answer the questions, but my world is on the page
and inside my head. When I grow up
I know I'll have my own life.

Shore

If I could walk on ice, with my feet bare,
I would feel all the spidery cracks spreading across the lake,
like a seismograph absorbing the snaking lines,
triggering Speed Up as I pass ice-fishing huts
decorated for the season,
red and green lights pulsing with the generators' groans.
Inside, men kneel over holes, clutch their sweating flasks,
waiting for something to rise.

Like Hermes, I glide on in my bare feet,
all silver, little wisps of snow nuzzling my ankles.
Halfway, there's no sense turning back.
In a cap with ear muffs, down coat, wool pants,
I'm warm, my feet a burnished sculpture,
or Adam's in a Flemish painting, glowing prehensile toes
gripping the frame.

All around me the lake's a dream catcher
I have slipped through and reached the shore.
Above me the stars keep their distance,
undisturbed by my journey
or the moon's recent eclipse.

Blue Moon

On this side of the lake I look across to the veranda
of the Blue Moon, where she would be dancing
with someone, her back bent to his glistening palm.

Phrases of a Latin tune carry across the water,
and lights clinging to the trellis wink on and off.
I can almost see her in her shining gown

moving smoothly across the dusty floor,
and conjure her expression—hungry? amused?
She always held something back.

Even with her head on my shoulder, I could see—
as in a mirror—her eyes roving the crowd.
I'd send a letter in a fish if I could,

a persistent fish, flopping a wet trail
through the couples to her, scales
glittering like the spinning ball overhead,

then fluttering on its tail to gasp out
my silver message, its frantic mouth
pulsing at her eager ear.

Pike

When a pike strikes you know it,
and sense you're being pulled on the glassy surface
of a cold lake in northern Minnesota far from shore
tethered to something prehistoric,
a toothed spear cleaving the water.
You want to cut the line, but it's clear down there.
You plunge over the gunwale, rod stretched before you,
thumb on the reel, eyes wide,
hair streaming behind like a myth,
and pursue the blade of a fish
to the bottom. The lake is a cloud overhead
and pours in when you open your mouth to sing.

II.

Pacific Slope

The Meadow

It's warm here tonight
in the western part of our country.
Nothing apocalyptic can happen
without foreshadowing.

Where do things go now
that gravity is broken
and the meadow tips up
like an emptying grain wagon?

The meadow narrows into night.
Things not rooted funnel
like crystals urged into a vial
by an insistent finger.

It's just a trick of the failing light.
Nothing is slipping away.
Tomorrow the sun will glint off dewy grass
as if nothing has happened.

Keepsake

All stones look rich when wet,
when the wave-end laps over them,
and they lie in a little trough of sand,
glistening ebony, dark orange,
or gray with a white seam.

When you rub the sand off and they dry,
they become ordinary,
except that they come
from the sea
which has worked them ceaselessly.

You keep bending,
certain you'll want to keep the next one,
a flawless, smooth pebble
that draws heat from your hand,
a little anchor
steadying you above the deep.

Pacific Coast

On the beach, the sun pressed down
compressing her flip-flops to wafers.
Air shrieked from her rubber raft.
Even her romance novel was suddenly abridged.

When her head cleared, she saw the sea completely still—
fishing boats with their long arms frozen.
High above a condor soared like an enormous kite,
head pivoting from side to side.
They *have* made a comeback, she thought,
brushed off the sand, and gathered up her stuff.

When she climbed the last dune to the PCH,
as usual, big cars roared by in a streak,
drivers with their Bluetooth ear pieces
glancing to reference her bikini.
For an instant their lips stopped moving.

She watched for a time,
wondering where everyone could be going.
What possible reason could they have
driving with such determination, while she . . .

She looked up. The condor had disappeared,
leaving a tiny vent in the blue.
She pushed the remote button and the Beetle squealed.
Behind the wheel, she rested her bare feet on the pedals,
started the engine, and swung onto the highway.
The sunroof slid open.

Primary Season

Now that the tree has come down
and sprawls in the yard for the Boy Scouts,
the officious eye of the TV, no longer reflecting
angels and colored lights, studies us
as we watch the early returns.

Bubble lights and plastic greens from the mantel
are packed beside the plump little birds and crèche.
All rest on a high shelf in the garage
with other once-a-year stuff—tax returns,
fading Easter baskets, a phosphorescent skeleton
folded like a contortionist.

We are well into the new year, its resolutions
and claims. The squabbling moves from Jobs to Race,
Walls to Coal to Immigrants, and always The Economy.
We watch from our couch. The holidays are over.

Church Street

We live on the darkest street in town.
At dusk the streetlight makes an effort,
loses its nerve, then fades out.
There are no churches.

My wife can't sleep. She moves
by braille in the study facing the street,
where headlights rove up and down the hill
illuminating parked cars and campaign signs.

I suppose it's a comfort knowing people
are pursuing some destination,
some streaming vision
out there in the dark.

Castoffs

Lifting my head I gaze at the moon
littered with castoffs from astronauts
traveling light on reentry.

The moon isn't far anymore.
In hermetic suits, men have
driven rovers and golf balls,
staked their claim with a rigid flag.

Though reflected, moonlight
is purer than its source these nights,
glinting off the snow, off crystals rising in the air—
turning us ghostly in our beds.

Backyard

1.
Out the window light slants
into late afternoon.
I can barely tell the blue from white lanterns
hanging in the trees.

Celebrating's over, past time
for them to come down,
but no ladders for me.
A cane's my prop this season.

Behind the cedar, which draws
the darkness first, the sky
is still clear for the moon's eclipse.
Even in the earth's shadow it's there.

2.
From the deck,
through maple branches,
I watch the stars pick their way—
clear, cold, and distant.

Snow covers the foothills.
On the mountain a string of lights
marks the ski runs—
a familiar constellation.

3.
Evening approaches and the sun
softens hills across the freeway.
Up the ravine Mt. Ashland
leans back against the sky.

Our backyard birch glows silver
before the darkening,
and the deck lights
throw a faint circle on the steps.

4.

This morning, the sun rose
above the garage; an orange moon
lingered in the northwest. February,
and the tips of the maple begin to swell.

Mid-May

The leaves are all out now
but for the tops of our dying birches.
We'll hold onto them one more season.
Green that bordered the dogwood blossoms
has taken over and the petals rust the ground.

It has rained off and on for three days,
with one downpour like those in Minnesota
when the barnyard potholes fill with water
and field work is suspended.

We're luxuriating in the wet
and have turned off the irrigation, hoping to bank it for August.
When the sun appears steam rises from the deck.
The air smells fresh, as if the world is starting over,
even greener this time.

Air Conditioning

I've opened up the house, smoke still in my nostrils.
For the first time in days I can see the foothills across the valley.
The fire seventy miles away grows,
and a small army grapples to contain it.

A scrub jay in the bird bath seems to beseech something
when it stretches its neck so water can run down its throat.
How are its lungs, I wonder,
as it glides to the cedar tree.

I fall into a pattern of opening the windows
for a few hours early in the day, then closing them
when the air smells like a bonfire.
We depend on systems to get through.

Air recirculates through filters, down ducts,
across the condenser, then flows again into our rooms
where we sit in our chairs, blankets covering our legs.
It's artificial I know, but it's how we live now.

Autumnal

The bronze birch borers have prevailed.
The backyard trees are down,
cut to lengths, and driven away.

Light has rushed in, and chrysanthemums
have room to throw their muted colors
and cold odor, a bitterness
that suits the close of something.

Late bloomers, funereal
after those fickle hot weather flowers,
prodigals that get lost in the racket of an easy life.

Mums face a low sun,
burdened with livening the season,
only to fade, turn frail and translucent,
stems pruned to stubble.

Apocalypse

Suppose it's fall and you're out walking
stiff-legged to rustle the leaves.

Color remains in the trees—ginkgos turned to pure yellow,
liquid ambers maroon where the sun hits first,
then descends through yellow
to pale green on the lowest branches.

Field binoculars hang around your neck,
which aches from watching waxwings
harvest berries on a mountain ash.

Suppose you notice clouds building,
darkening to a color more ominous
than the green sky of imminent tornados
on the prairies in your youth.

You're certain the end of something is near,
and turn again to the silky, gleaning birds,
who, making their thin call, suddenly
lift off.

Vision

I retired to the edge of a forest.
That way I could keep an eye
on the owls and become wise.

I stayed up nights
and hunted voles,
but never caught one.

My night vision isn't good;
my head turns only so far.
I looked up as the owls

spread their wings and left roosts,
wind brushing through
their feathers.

They never touched branches,
gliding toward their prey,
while, on all fours, I snapped twigs.

They grew used to me, but hunted
in other parts of the forest,
leaving me to stagger back to my tent.

What did I learn? That I was no good
as an owl. That scrabbling on all fours
is hard on the knees and shreds your jeans.

That during the day I saw better,
but never saw owls. That owls
make use of what they've become.

Tracks

Fresh tiger tracks in the mud
writes the hermit Stonehouse
hundreds of years ago in China.
Few poets can attest to that spoor.

Are tigers still there in the mountains
between Huzhou and Hangzhou?

What I have to offer on Church Street
are junco turds on the deck railings,
deer pellets on the driveway,
raccoon nails etched in an icy puddle.

In the foothills of the Siskiyous,
wide pads of the mountain lion,
black bear slashes on fir trees.

Creeks run through town—trout,
herons, the resilient ouzel. On the paths
people restrain their pets, plastic bag
in one hand, leash in the other.

Deeper

To learn where the wild ducks fly
you have to behave like a duck.
Lose your fear of water,
dabble your bill in the lake,
then bob head first, butt in the air,
like a green-winged teal.

To live like a diving duck is another matter—
a merganser, say, one with teeth—
you have to go deep, search the bottom.
It gets darker and colder the deeper you go.

Who knows what you'll find down there,
but if it changes your life, you're not a duck.

The Routine at Stonesthrow Ranch

At sunup the rooster sidles down
the little wooden ramp, head cocked
over his shoulder, one wicked eye
on the treetop, the other at the ground.

He flaps his rusty wings two, three times,
thrusts out his chest, drags his spurs to stay earthbound,
and crows all clear. Five hens squawk
down the gangplank and run stiffly to the feeder.

Then a young black lab is urged inside the fence.
The answer to hawk depredation, he eats chicken feed,
ignores the rooster, and follows the hens all day,
inching under the coop to nap, a flat, black shape down there.

Long after shadows reach across the coop yard,
the dog is let out. The chickens retire to their roosts
and settle down over their feet. The red-tailed hawk
rocks high in the cedar. *The chicken coop is shut up tight.*

Open

The dog with her head out the car window,
ears swept back, nose taking it all in,
is not thinking about needing to write it down
before it gets away. It comes to her in a flood.
We can see the grin on her face.

Cee Cee gets lonely in the pasture all day,
wearing his filthy winter blanket, lipping the brown grass.
When we pull down the drive, he acknowledges us with a snort,
trots to the fence, and presents his long face
for a rub along the blaze.

For fleeting moments our lives are Now,
but then niggling regrets, envies, longings intrude.
We know the end is out there, but when,
and how? Maybe the animals, with their steady gaze,
can teach us.

III.

Afield

Ancient Ones

Suppose they didn't disappear,
didn't migrate to pueblos,
didn't leave their rock dwellings
tucked in alcoves in nearly every canyon
on the Colorado Plateau.

Suppose it rained those dry years
a gentle, long, female rain,
and their crops flourished below
along the streams and rivers—
corn and squash glistening
against the red rocks.

On their knees women
ground corn on hollowed stones,
children chased turkeys
hopping ahead, restrained
by their tethers.

Men on ladders blew red powder
over their spread hands, or picked
great coils, grids, meandering lines,
and the ghostly figures with antennae
sprouting from their heads.
In their midst the audacious, bent figure
of Water Sprinkler playing his flute.

When the Spanish arrived on their horses,
the People looked down from ledges,
stunned by beasts their art
could not accommodate.

What the Dead Miss

The dead miss out on everything
after they go underground
or on a shelf in the closet.

It matters only to the living,
who wish the dead could see the new baby,
the Giants sweep the Series,
results of the recent election
and hurricane.

It would be nice perhaps,
but the globe would get packed,
the dead hanging around to witness
what happens next.

We may miss them,
but the dead don't miss us.
They drift into the past,
become fainter and fainter.

We know less and less of them
as the boundary thins
and we close in on
what they know.

Goodbye to the Tears

Beads fall from a broken necklace.
On all fours I scrabble to corral them,
to find every one to restring.
I like to keep them handy.

Under the fridge,
between the boards into layers of sub-flooring,
to all corners of the room they've rolled,
balls of mercury or thick blood,
altering as I grasp them,
masters of avoidance.

They're not precious, but hard to come by,
and I may need some in the future.
You get only so many.

Call

The cell phone trembles in his breast pocket.
"God almighty," he says, but isn't sure it's a prayer
or a curse. It's AFib again, he thinks,
and, beginning to sweat, sits down on a bench.
He urges the phone from its pocket,
handles it carefully, like an animal, maybe,
something the cat shouldn't tangle with.
He pushes "Accept" and holds the phone
near his ear. "Speak to me," he says.

Legacy

The dead from ruined villages'
dark thoughts wander the mined roads,
are driven through the night by blasts
and keening so high only the dogs
hear it and join in.

Those cries haunt the living
who carry the dead through
the marketplace to the burying ground
spread beyond its walls,
the earth so loose it collapses
in the open graves.

The infected thoughts of the living
cannot be appeased or interred.

They survive everything.

Insomnia

Why does it come to mind now?
It happened fifty years ago.

It wasn't so bad then—
something blurted that hurt,
but didn't maim.

My mother said I had a sharp tongue,
said she always loved me,
but sometimes didn't like me.

Through the open patio door
I hear rain strike the maple leaves.

I'm tired. My mind is just searching
for something to blame me for.

Hostage

The moon is the hub of the mind.

That's why you can't sleep
when it's full, and the light
streams into the room
and takes you hostage

with a pull so great the bed
lifts and you're weightless.
Reflection is subtle.
Pale light probes.

Any thought you have
now lasts, though the moon
will become a sliver,
nights darker.

Out your window the shrubs
strain from their shadows,
and birds get no rest,
eyes dry from watching.

Next day you'll move
lazily, musing "Daylight
is brutal," and keep
to the shady side of the street.

What has become of you
you're not sure, but know change,
as if moonlight has invaded your marrow,
and cells stream from your bones.

Redrock

Some say
once there was a face,
maybe an Ancient One,
but it's worn away.

Wind and snow and rain.

Sandstone dissolves slowly
but fast for rock.

Grit sifts into my pockets.
Grit in my teeth tastes good,
like the desert,
substantial and spacious,
on the move.

I never trusted that face.

A thing should be what it is.
It should absorb the heat,
take in the rain and snow,
become darker red when wet
and from a slanting sun.

It should grip my soles
when I walk.

Recent Reading

I lie on my back, pillow under my knees.
The clock reads 2:23, and I know it's accurate,
atomic, picking up waves from Denver.
The deck lights clicked off three hours ago.
The moon is new.

I could switch on the bed lamp and read.
The Liberator, Simón Bolívar, past his usefulness
to politicians, near death from TB and exhaustion,
is on his last journey. He'll not make the packet boat to France—
I've seen his chronology at the end. And now
the author is dead, too, nearly two centuries later.

Raccoons snuffle in the flower garden.
New leaves on the maple shiver from exposure.
The book ends with Bolívar's death, but I'll finish it
anyway; the plot doesn't matter.

I open the book. Bolívar is in Cartagena,
in a hammock, chilled, sweating with fever.
The revolution wasn't worth shit he tells his servant.

Silk

Their robes were light and their horses well-fed.
That much was clear when they came into the firelight.
Silk can keep you warm, even when soiled.

Embroidered horses milled about, riders
with raised swords, banners, armored men on foot
marched out of sight.

The wearers' faces were drawn, unfamiliar—
traders with nothing to trade. I rose to greet them
and offer food. Anything to hear their story.

The Words

*And are we here,
perhaps merely to say: house, bridge, fountain,
gate, jar, fruit tree, window—*

Rilke was hesitant—*perhaps, merely*—
but his choices were exact, as if he were Adam
occupied in naming. *Fruit tree.* Does saying it
make the serpent coil around a branch?

That Rilke set these words down to rub against each other
makes them shimmer. But why not *pen, flame, gable,
rock, air, robin, storefront*? Or *threshold, post, desk,
horse, loam, glacier, oak*?

We are here for a short time,
but these things we have lived in, crossed over,
wished on, opened on rusty hinges, drunk from,
and gazed through into the orchard.

Portal

Beside a purple bus on the plain
of the Knight of the Sorrowful Countenance,
tourists in shorts and shirts with too many pockets
await me, luggage lined up like robots,
while I've sprung through a portal to some other country,
not the one with bullrings, sherry, and *duende*.

In the Himalayas, the euros in my money belt are worthless,
Tilley hat absurd, and I'm cold postholing across a snowfield,
plunging my stick into the upslope to avoid sliding into a crevasse
and disappearing forever down an icy shaft.

Far down the mountain,
in a compound in deep shadows violating laws of the sun,
monks in red robes scurry along breezeways
on the urgent business of prolonging mysteries.

I'd give anything to be there finding myself,
but looking down makes me dizzy,
and I'm busy breaking trail,
trying to find my way back
by planes, whose doors seal with sighs,
then trains that don't leave the station,
just whistle long and hulk in steam.

Back in La Mancha the travelers stand by the bus,
monitors at summer camp,
hands shading their eyes, gazing at windmills,
cameras dangling from lanyards around their ropy necks.

They'll break into groups and take pictures of one another,
then stare at the backs of their cameras
to see how they turned out.

Outlet

Don't stay here even if other hotels are full.
Terrible reception, sheets your heels rip,
a bedspread you wouldn't lie on. Carpet?
Unspeakable. The beds are bad, the food worse,
the help worse yet. They nod Yes sir,
right away, sir, and you never see them again,
though you may spy one or two lighting up
in the shrubs by the car park.

You're on your own. You don't mind.
It's easier to do it yourself anyway.
As long as you have the room, you can hide out.
You have plenty to do, and your plug fits the outlet,
not always the case in your travels. You can lie down,
take a nap—avoidance and renewal at the same time.

You may start thinking about your life—things
done and undone—and writing high school classmates
you slighted forty years ago. The fat girl dying
to dance with you. The boy you turned on
to stay in the crowd. Take my advice: Don't stay here.
It'll get in your head.

Parallel

He strides along the embankment.
The river has been straightened and lined.
Sandbags squat atop the wall.

Rain falls on him, then doesn't as he
passes under trees through shadows
and into the wet glow from streetlights.

Outside the city, deer come to drink,
nightbirds dive and cry. The river flows across fields,
finds its way. He hopes he can do the same,
as he walks through wet and dry, light and dark.

Stonework

As you grew up you knew your town—
the pool hall across from the grain elevator,
the Chevy Garage on Highway 14 by the Red Rooster Cafe.

When you moved to a city where the work was
you were lost. Tall buildings blocked the view,
endless grids. You wandered,
and found a route to a job
where you cut rectangular holes in marble slabs
for sinks to slide into.

You loved the shop. Slabs leaned against the walls,
fat leaves of a giant book, smooth and solid.
It seemed a sin to cut holes in them but you did,
and began taking to your room the marble you cut out,
heavy, but like maps with roads or rivers,
or tablets come down from the mountain.

You traced their twisting lines
that merged with others that faded away,
or were cut off at the edges.
They didn't help you find your way in the city,
but helped you find the way in your head.

Over time they piled up in your room
so thick the floor began to bow.
You loved to rub them—cool to the touch
with just enough resistance.

Carrara you said to yourself,
the melodic sound of the quarry
away off on another continent—
a woman's name, exotic,
and out of reach.

Implications

She said she was escaping her life,
and needed gas money and that's why
she picked him up. His pack was stowed
in the back across a cardboard box. Beside it
a gray, tiger-striped cat slumped in a cage.

He knew there was only one way to escape
your life. No denying that. Even in trying,
your life is your life. But he didn't say so.

The car, a faded blue Mazda,
smelled of cigarettes and French fries.
He looked ahead at the road stretching
straight before them like a sentence.
After a while he asked the expected.

"Oh, the usual," she said. "A man who drank often
and too much and worked too seldom.
My story isn't a new one, but it's the one I have."
Her voice was flat, like the center of the country.

He admired her tone, that way with words.
He looked at her profile. Her mouth and hair
drooped with fatigue, he thought,
and her T-shirt was soiled.

Her hands gripped the steering wheel,
and she kept her eyes on the road.
"What do you call the cat?" he said.

Watcher

What if she ran screaming from her house?—
the girl at the end of the street,
the one with no mother,
the one you watched at school
as she passed solitary in the hall
with her back straight, books clutched to her chest,
face composed as if determined
to make the best of it—
or two rows over in the classroom
with her dark hair draped over her notebook,
unaware of your vigil.

And when you saw her at lunch, alone,
with her pitiful paper sack,
what then?
Did you go and lean casually on the table
and speak to her, use small talk
even though you knew small talk
wouldn't interest her.
Or did you sit down beside her
and extend half a sandwich
and wait?

Would you rush down the street
to her now, ask her what's wrong,
put your arms around her,
tell her she's safe with you?

Lost

The idea of a map is to keep us from becoming lost,
writes the naturalist, now without a chart in the underworld.

The redrock Southwest is like the home of the dead—
dangerous, hot, and bewitching.

Hades, a shrewd judge of character, figured brash Orpheus,
who knew his way out, would have to look back.
Perhaps he heard the descending song of the canyon wren.

I like maps, the kind that fold, soften, tear at the creases,
and begin to look like the snowflakes you cut out in school—
a world spread out on your lap as you travel from Crownpoint
to Shiprock. You mark it until the Four Corners becomes a web.

There's a knack for getting lost, says the poet, who was talking
about writing. Just set out—you're better off without a guide.

IV.

Return

Return

It was dark on the old street
lined with elms. I stood on tiptoe
at the front door, and stared through the slim windows.
The long hallway was dim,
and branched off to the girls' room.

For years they complained about each other's habits,
and drew a line down the middle,
but when it came time,
neither would take the bedroom I left.

Water ran in the pipes.
I listened to the clatter of plates in the sink,
mother cleaning up after supper.
She worked alone.

As I pored over math problems in my spot at the dinner table,
I could hear her hum "Unchained Melody."
In his living room easy chair,
father scanned tomorrow's punch list for the building site.

How calm, how ordered it seemed,
but I couldn't open the door.
There was no knob and I wasn't Christ.
My hand traced the scratch marks of our last dog
buried under the hedge.

Cold Spell

Snow piled up on the branches.
We could hear some crack late at night
when the temp fell into single digits,
unusual out here near the Pacific.

Rhododendron leaves curled into themselves
almost to needles. All night we let the faucet
send a slender stream into the sink.

The first two days after surgery
I didn't care if I died.
I felt the sap freezing in my arm as I repositioned,
waiting for the snap. It seemed right,
my life matching the season,
but the furnace in the crawl space kept huffing away,
pushing warm air up through the ducts.
Not a time to freeze from inside
and out.

On pills my brain stretched out like the Dakotas
with a blizzard slicing through, scouring the land,
smashing into frail sheds thrown up
out there miles beyond lights.
It was not unpleasant.

Then I returned to my life of desires,
saltines, and cold drinks.
The rhody leaves unfurled,
snow tumbled from the cedar onto cars
spinning up our street.

Ticking

One thing opens then closes
almost on its own, as your hand
when you catch a ball.

Seconds, minutes, hours, weeks,
one year ends and another begins—
your life ticking along.

Once you were the youngest on the team,
last chosen and exiled to right field.
Now you're the oldest, feeling lucky,
but a little tired, and you can't turn your neck
as you back down the drive.

Tinnitus

My ears no longer long for sound.
I carry sound in my head—
like static when snowstorms
bury the FM translator on Grizzly Peak.
A doctor said no tumor broadcasts in my brain,
so I'm not afraid and never lonely,
but seldom listen to music.
White noise occupies *that* space
the way bees swarm a hive.

There are times when my attention drifts
and it retreats,
as those living near a freeway
ignore the drone of traffic.
If I think of what it might advise,
it comes back, murmuring my name—
a great comfort in the middle of the night,
drowning out the furnace ticking
in the crawl space,
the grinding of arthritic joists above.
I relax on the little ice floe of my bed
and await further reports.

Calling

Honking geese at night remind me of home.
After milking, we sat at the table eating supper
and heard geese flying south. In the fog they seemed so close
their calls plunged through the roof. In that yellow kitchen
with its wood stove, we shivered. I knew calling
kept them together in that vee passing overhead,
but the answers were thin out there miles from town.

The farmhouse is gone now, my parents, too.
What do the geese tell each other for comfort?
And how long can they stay up there before fatigue
brings them down to some farmer's half-picked field?

Rust

Driving to Home Depot for hinges,
I pass an old pear orchard behind the Peterbilt Sales and Service.
The trees still produce, or those acres
would anchor the new La-Z-Boy superstore
a quarter mile on.

Last year's growth is a lovely reddish-rust,
like the eyes of a Great Horned Owl,
a shade my mother favored, reflecting her chosen season,
and the rust of weeds in the ditches,
and the soybean fields nearing harvest.

In a framed photo she wears a rust dress
with white collar and cuffs—a Butte Knit I bought her—
and a brooch of tiny fall leaves.
My father, in a brown and rust sport coat
she must have bought him,
smiles anyway.

On their right my favorite aunt and uncle,
the ones who drank and smoked, and danced out at the lake,
wear burgundy and blue.

Behind them all it's autumn at Garvin Park,
with yellow leaves out of focus.

My mother, who died in the fall,
lies in her coffin in a dress of pastel blues and pinks,
ready for spring and the resurrection.

The pear orchard's twisted, black trunks and rust-colored branches
will bear for a few more years
before giving way to what they're zoned for.

Work

I, too, have sat by someone's deathbed
and looked into her face in the last hours.
Though her eyes were open she didn't see,
being intent on something else.

Each flying petal diminishes the spring.
Her breathing was harsh; it went on and on—
hard work even for someone used to hard work.
Then it became still, and the work was left to me.

Endings

My father knew what the end looks like.
He found it after my mother died.
Her mind gone, she didn't know what it was,
but she understood something,
and quit eating and drinking.

As she lay on a narrow bed
we held her hands; her fingers
felt like twigs peeled of bark.
She rasped, then she didn't,
and we closed her eyes.

Four months later my father
sent us home, his mind set
on what he had to accomplish.
When we left the dim room
he lay, eyes closed,
hands folded on his chest,
as if he were already practicing.

Siblings in August

Judy's hair is soft as a puppy's.
They all rub her head.
She's tan and in remission.
They're sitting around the table on the patio,
and it's hot, but there's a hint of a breeze.
The mosquitos aren't bad,
and the crickets are sawing away,
one in particular
that must be in a flower box.

The siblings are telling family stories,
but the events aren't the same
in memory and everyone laughs.
All agree that Paul was incorrigible
and had a room of his own
the size of a closet,
while the others slept in another room,
and Sally was sweet
and sorely put upon by Paul,
but she adored him,
and Patty was the oldest and went away
and missed much of what draws
the rest to Pullman,
and Judy was the baby.

It begins to get dark.
There is a full moon, a blue one,
and the crickets roar louder.
Around the table they all know
good luck when they hear it.

Decluttering

Katherine drove three boxes of books to the library.
Her friend had died
and Katherine cleared the bookshelves in the bedroom.
She'd already taken clothes to Goodwill,
kept a couple of sweaters for herself, hardly worn,
but that was all. She couldn't bear the thought
of stepping into her friend's dresses.

She pulled onto the striped area between two handicapped spots,
reserved for vans whose ramps snake out their sliding doors.
By policy she wouldn't park there,
even to dash in for a book held at the counter.
But the boxes were heavy; she'd need someone to lift them.

She popped the trunk and scanned the titles on the spines.
She'd rushed packing them, just slid them into the shallow boxes,
adjusting so every space was filled exactly.
She'd always had that knack—packing a suitcase,
cooler, grocery bag. It was satisfying seeing ahead
how everything could fit, almost with a click.

And now her friend was dead
and Katherine was doing what was needed.
There would be room on the library shelves for most of the books,
but some would go on the sale tables.
She took two, *War and Peace* and *Moby-Dick*.

She liked big books with big stories.
And if one became tired of the plot
(How long would it take Pierre and Natasha to get together?
Would Ahab ever encounter the whale?),
one could read chapters that weren't made up,
about the Battle of Austerlitz
or cetology.

Sometimes it helped to tamp down the imagination.
She put the two volumes on the passenger seat,
left the car running, and went to get help with the boxes.

Element

Once I was a child gliding
arm over arm across the lake.
Sun glinted off the water.
The sky was brilliant and deep.

With each breath I squinted at the dock
which receded into green lawns
and trees on the bank. White-sided houses
on wood foundations stared out.

Every summer my parents rented one,
then dozed, mixed drinks,
or thumbed through magazines,
stunned by vacation indolence.

I was alone stroking on,
beginning to tire, akin to no element.
Not even the land would hold me up
if I could get there.

When I reached the diving platform
a hundred yards from shore,
I pulled myself up by my arms starting to muscle,
and lay back on the warped boards.

As the sun dried me, I looked into the sky
arcing over the lake. The platform rocked,
constrained by its tether. I was alone in the universe,
warm in my blue trunks, and fell asleep.

Empathy

Life is easy
if you don't feel too much,
and if you have enough money
to dine out when you want to—
with a bottle of wine.

My range is now
between twelve and fifteen dollars retail.
Before the settlement
I stopped at ten.

Now I sit on my back deck.
It's unseasonably hot,
record-breaking.

The tulip petals bend over backwards,
unattractive, but in the evening
discreet in yellow skirts.

I'm reading a poem about the writer's pain
when his mother died.

I can feel his, but not mine.
It seems so long ago.

Encounter

Say that the wind was more than you could take
    and the sun shone in your eyes
    and you could not see what was coming
    and you were afraid.

Say that the wind died and a cloud covered the sun
    and you saw nothing was coming
    and you were afraid that nothing would ever come
    and your life would be wasted.

Say that you kept going because that's what you do
    and there was always the hope
    that something would smash into you
    and give your life value
    for then you would suffer.

Say you did suffer anyway and then you died
    and your loved ones followed your hearse
    in long black cars with the headlights shining
    down the road perpendicular to the town
    and through the gate into the graveyard.

Say for you there was nothing to worry about
    and you missed out on the beauty
    of the place where you were laid to rest,
    the trees and flowers and birds and fields
    and the water tower in the distance
    and what you longed for was always present
    and in front of you.

Wings

As a kid I wanted to spread my wings,
so I built them out of balsa wood
and the kind of tissue paper
used in kites from Ben Franklin.
I nailed a wood frame and glued on paper.
The hardest part was the harness—
cut from the reins of our long-gone work horses—
which had to be tight so the wings
felt part of me, but hinged for flapping.

When I plunged off the peak of the chicken coop,
I flapped them twice, lost altitude
and crashed, snapping the frame
and my forearm.

Gliding wasn't flying exactly,
but the next best thing,
and building the wings was easier—
just one long, flat frame with paper strapped to my back,
so when I dove off the roof, arms stuck out
like Superman's, it would hold me up.
I would glide who knew how far, and return to earth,
alighting like a feather.
That was the theory.

In practice, what's the point of describing it.
I did descend in a sort of angle to the ground
some distance from the coop,
but landed like sliding head first into third base.
Scraped and bleeding, humiliated,
I gave up flight, and spent the rest of my life behind a desk.

I've worked toward some meaning for this story,
but it doesn't have the dignity even of Icarus,
who failed because he was too successful,
and it went to his head.
His father was along, while mine was in the field on a tractor.
I should have been helping him,
not jumping off buildings. Instead of a point
about persistence, and elegance in defeat,
this story is, suddenly, about guilt.
And there it will stay.

Father and Son

Once again I bring up the myth of Icarus
a foolish young man flying too close to the sun,
and who can blame him
being airborne.

He forgot his father's warning as have all
who defy gravity
or leave home.

From below his father watched the boy
become a silhouette against the gleam,
then float by him
arms and legs flailing.

They may have locked eyes just for a second.
It was then Icarus thought what the poet suggests.

My father has deceived me.
His wings are real.

Then he became a speck against the waves,
and feathers fluttered past Daedalus
in a rocking motion
like falling leaves.

As I raked hay in the June sun or lifted off the chicken coop
in my balsa wood and tissue paper wings,
never did I think my father
betrayed me.

What kind of father did Icarus believe he had
to bring such a thought just before
he plunged into the Aegean.

Who can say what we consider at the last.

My father near the end
said he had no regrets about his life.
He liked being in the field,
liked planting and picking,
even liked cows.

As the days in the hospital dragged on
he told the minister

"I don't mind dying.
It's this farting around I can't stand."

When Daedalus saw Icarus fall,
he must have stopped beating his wings
in a frozen moment.
Maybe then he thought

*I'll follow my son and find him
beneath the water.*

However,
he began to wave his arms,
and, according to the myth,
flew on to Sicily.

Close

Let the evening hills share each other's sorrow.
At the coming dark the valleys will close,
squeezing the darkness, cold and pure
as the creeks above the grazing herd.
Nothing escapes. The hills rub their sides
against each other and the animals
dip their muzzles in the stream.
The souls of the dead are pressed thin,
vapor rising from the water.

Thirst

It's dark as I stand at the kitchen sink
filling my glass with my finger crooked over the edge.
I'm thirsty after dreams of the desert—
sand endless and blowing into new dunes
and across the railroad tracks
like the ones Lawrence blew up in the movie.
I saw him crouching at some distance,
both hands on the plunger.
It's a long time till dawn
with its rosy fingers
and dim responsibilities,
the first one being brushing my teeth.
Someone may want to kiss me.

Acreage

Beneath the frost line,
under the soil black as coal,
tile carries spring water to a ditch along the dump road
into a culvert and across a neighbor's field.

Where it ends up I don't know,
maybe miles away in the Des Moines River.

On this rainy, cool day I look west across the field,
not as flat as one might think,
with more than one catch basin,
spots too low to plant some years.

Soybeans' puny leaves urge through the crust
strewn with last year's cornstalks.

How many times have I been over this fifty acres?—

Bending near a flatbed piled with the yearly harvest of rocks
worked up by freeze and thaw.

Chopping out volunteer corn from ankle-high beans
with a hoe in May or later in summer with a machete.

Steering the Oliver and four-row cultivator
for the first cleaning, then the second,
then the laying by.

Notes

"Idle"—The italicized line is from *The Collected Songs of Cold Mountain*, translated by Red Pine (Copper Canyon Press).

"Perspective"—Prompted by W.S. Merwin's poem "Print Falling Out of Somewhere," from *The Rain in the Trees* (Knopf).

"Scene in Black and Gray"—Prompted by W.S. Merwin's poem, "History," in *The Rain in the Trees* (Knopf).

"Weight"—The italicized line is from *The Collected Songs of Cold Mountain*, translated by Red Pine (Copper Canyon Press).

"Shore"—The first line is from Carolyn Kizer's translations of Tu Fu in *Knock upon Silence* (University of Washington Press).

"Blue Moon"—The italicized line is from a poem by Yen Shu in *Poems of the Masters: China's Classic Anthology of T'ang and Sung Dynasty Verse*, translated by Red Pine (Copper Canyon Press).

"Castoffs"—The italicized line is from a poem by Li Pai in *Poems of the Masters: China's Classic Anthology of T'ang and Sung Dynasty Verse*, translated by Red Pine (Copper Canyon Press).

"Backyard"—For Erik Muller.

"Vision"—The italicized line is from *The Collected Songs of Cold Mountain*, translated by Red Pine (Copper Canyon Press).

"Tracks"—The italicized line is from #1 of *The Mountain Poems of Stonehouse*, translated by Red Pine (Copper Canyon Press).

"Deeper"—The italicized line is from *The Collected Songs of Cold Mountain*, translated by Red Pine (Copper Canyon Press).

"The Routine at Stonesthrow Ranch"—The italicized sentence is from a poem by Wang Chia in *Poems of the Masters: China's Classic Anthology of T'ang and Sung Dynasty Verse*, translated by Red Pine (Copper Canyon Press).

"Open"—Prompted by the line "Animals see the open with their whole eyes," from Rainer Maria Rilke's *Duino Elegies*, translated by Gary Miranda (Tavern Books).

"Legacy"—Prompted by Tu Fu's lines, "Those who've lost all for war, those on far/frontiers dead: they wander dark thoughts," from *Classic Chinese Poetry: An Anthology*, translated by David Hinton (Farrar, Straus and Giroux).

"Hostage"—The italicized line is from *The Collected Songs of Cold Mountain*, translated by Red Pine (Copper Canyon Press).

"Recent Reading"—The book and author are *The General in His Labyrinth* and Gabriel García Márquez.

"Silk"—The italicized line is from a poem by Tu Fu in *Poems of the Masters: China's Classic Anthology of T'ang and Sung Dynasty Verse*, translated by Red Pine (Copper Canyon Press).

"The Words"—The first stanza is from Rainer Maria Rilke's *Duino Elegies*, translated by Gary Miranda (Tavern Books).

"Outlet"—*Don't stay here* is from *The Collected Songs of Cold Mountain*, translated by Red Pine (Copper Canyon Press).

"Lost"—*The idea of a map is to keep us from becoming lost* is from *The Last Cheater's Waltz: Beauty and Violence in the Desert Southwest* (The University of Arizona Press) by Ellen Meloy. *There's a knack for getting lost* is from *The Answers Are Inside the Mountains* by William Stafford (The University of Michigan Press).

"Ticking"—The italicized line is from *The Collected Songs of Cold Mountain*, translated by Red Pine (Copper Canyon Press).

"Tinnitus"—Prompted by Robert Bly's line "The longing the ear feels for sound," in *Morning Poems* (HarperCollins).

"Calling"—The italicized line is from a poem by Ou-Yang Hsiu in *Poems of the Masters: China's Classic Anthology of T'ang and Sung Dynasty Verse*, translated by Red Pine (Copper Canyon Press).

"Work"—The italicized line is from a poem by Tu Fu in *Poems of the Masters: China's Classic Anthology of T'ang and Sung Dynasty Verse*, translated by Red Pine (Copper Canyon Press).

"Endings"—For Mike Kilpatrick (1933-2012).

"Siblings in August"—For Judy Busch.

"Father and Son"—Prompted by the lines "In the story, the boy, falling, must have thought his/father had wings/Unlike his own, & real," from Larry Levis' "As It Begins with a Brush Stroke on a Snare Drum" in *The Widening Spell of the Leaves* (University of Pittsburgh Press).

"Close"—The italicized line is from a poem by Ch'eng Hao in *Poems of the Masters: China's Classic Anthology of T'ang and Sung Dynasty Verse*, translated by Red Pine (Copper Canyon Press).

"Acreage"—For Seamus Heaney (1939-2013).

Credits and Acknowledgments

Thank you to Jonah Bornstein, Steve Dieffenbacher, Barry Grimes, Paul Merchant, Erik Muller, John Ruff, Peter Sears, Clemens Starck, and Patty Wixon for help with poems in this book, and to the following publications in which poems in *Laying By* first appeared, sometimes in slightly different form:

Cascadia Review: "Drive-by," "Church Street," "Open," "The Words"
Cloudbank: "Empathy"
The Cresset: "Bethel Cemetery," "Watcher," "Tinnitus"
Elohi Gadugi Journal: "Shore," "Legacy," "Portal," "Return"
The Enigmatist: "What the Dead Miss"
Hubbub: "Fall Plowing," "Goodbye to the Tears," "Wings"
Jefferson Monthly: "Cold Spell"
Midwest Review: "The Meadow," "Apocalypse"
Valparaiso Poetry Review: "Stonework"
Windfall: "Backyard," "Air Conditioning," "Autumnal," "Tracks," "Rust"

"Lost" was published in *A Ritual to Read to Each Other: Poems in Conversation with William Stafford*, edited by Becca J.R. Lachman (Woodley Press).

Fourteen poems appeared in the chapbook *Blue Moon: Poems from Chinese Lines*, published by Wordcraft of Oregon in 2010.

Author's Biography

Vincent Wixon grew up in Minnesota, but has lived in the West for over forty years. His previous collections of poems are *Blue Moon: Poems from Chinese Lines* (Wordcraft of Oregon, 2010), *The Square Grove* (Traprock Books, 2006), and *Seed* (May Day Press, 1993). His poem "Tornado Weather" appears in Garrison Keillor's anthology, *Good Poems, American Places*. He is coproducer of videos on William Stafford and Lawson Inada. For many years he was a scholar in the William Stafford Archives at Lewis & Clark College, and, with former Archives director Paul Merchant, has edited four books by Stafford, including *Sound of the Ax: Aphorisms and Poems*, published in the Pitt Poetry Series. In 2014, Vincent and his wife Patty received the Stewart H. Holbrook Literary Legacy Award for contributions to the literary life of Oregon.

www.ingramcontent.com/pod-product-compliance
Lightning Source LLC
Chambersburg PA
CBHW050330120526
44592CB00014B/2119